THE ART AND SECRET OF POSITIVE THINKING

DEVELOPING A POSITIVE ATTITUDE FOR SUCCESS

DR. JAGADEESH PILLAI

Made with ♥ on the Notion Press Platform
www.notionpress.com

|| Dedicated to all wisdom seekers around the world ||

Contents

Contents

Prayer

"Om Poornamadah Poornamidam Poornat Poornamudachyate,Poornasya Poornamaadaya Poornamevavashishyate,Om Shantih, Shantih, Shantih"

The literal interpretation of this mantra is: That which is Absolute, This which is Absolute, Absolute arises from Absolute, If Absolute is removed from Absolute, Absolute remains

OM Peace, Peace, Peace.

About The Author

Dr. Jagadeesh Pillai is a renowned Guinness World Record holder, writer, and researcher hailing from Varanasi, also known as the abode of Lord Shiva. With a Ph.D. in Vedic Science and a range of creative ideas and achievements, he is a true polymath. He is the author of more than 100 books including Research Publications. Although his roots can be traced back to Kerala, the people of Varanasi hold him in high regard and affectionately consider him one of their own.

Dr. Pillai has achieved four Guinness World Records in the following subjects:

"Script to Screen" - In this record, Dr. Pillai produced and directed an animation film within the shortest time possible, breaking the previous record set by Canadians. He has also received numerous national and international awards and recognitions for this achievement.

Longest Line of Postcards - For this record, Dr. Pillai created a line of 16,300 postcards on the occasion of the 163rd anniversary of Indian Postal Day. The event also included a questionnaire about the Indian flag.

Largest Poster Awareness Campaign - Dr. Pillai designed an awareness campaign on the subject of "Beti Bachao - Beti Padhao" (Save the Girl Child - Educate the Girl Child) to achieve this record.

Largest Envelope - In tribute to the Indian Prime Minister's

"Make in India" initiative, Dr. Pillai created a 4000 square meter envelope using waste paper to achieve this record.

Attempted - **70000 Candles on a 210 kg Cake** - To celebrate the 70th Indian Independence Day, Dr. Pillai attempted to light 70,000 candles on a 210 kg cake, which was recorded in World Records India.

Attempted - **Documentary on Dhamek Stupa of Sarnath in 17 Languages** - Dr. Pillai attempted to create a documentary on the Dhamek Stupa of Sarnath, dubbing it in 17 different languages. The result of this attempt is currently awaiting confirmation from the Guinness World Records.

Dr. Pillai is skilled in teaching the Bhagavad Gita, a Hindu scripture, and is popular among young people. He has helped many young people improve their lives through his motivational teachings.

In addition to teaching, he has composed and sung numerous Sanskrit Bhajans and patriotic songs.

He has also written and directed several short films and documentaries for awareness campaigns, and has volunteered with the police in both UP and Kerala to spread awareness about various issues through videos and photography.

Incredibly, he has produced and directed over 100 documentaries about the city of Varanasi, all on his own.

He has also helped and guided more than 25 boys and girls to achieve world records through creative and innovative methods. He is a multifaceted person who uses his intellect and the blessings given to him by God to excel in various areas. He is both a teacher and a student, always learning and teaching, and is able to master any subject he comes across.

He is a selfless social activist and motivational speaker who has overcome struggles and failures to become a successful and enthusiastic individual with a rich life experience.

In addition to his work with the Bhagavad Gita, he is also an efficient Tarot card reader, Astro-Vastu consultant, and a talented singer and composer. He has sung the entire Ram Charita Manas and Bhagavad Gita in his own compositions, and has sung the phrase "Lokah Samastha Sukhino Bhavantu" in 50 different languages. He is currently working on a detailed and scientific study of Vedas, Upanishads, Puranas, and the Bhagavad Gita. He has also composed and sung the Hanuman Chalisa and Gayatri Mantra in 108 and 1008 different compositions, respectively.

Awards - Four Times Guinness World Records, Winner of Mahatma Gandhi Vishwa Shanti Puraskar, Mahatma Gandhi Global Peace Ambassador, Kashi Ratna Award, Dr. APJ Abdul Kalam Motivational Person of the Year 2017, Mother Teresa Award, Indira Gandhi Priyadarshini Award, Bharat Vikas Ratna Award, Udyog Ratna Award, Vigyan Prasar Award, Poorvanchal Ratn Samman.

Preface

Welcome to The Art and Secrets of Positive Thinking: Developing a Positive Attitude for Success! In this book, we will explore the power of positive thinking and how it can help us achieve success in life. We will discuss the importance of cultivating a positive attitude and how to do it effectively. We will also look at the benefits of positive thinking and how to use it to our advantage. Finally, we will look at the practical steps you can take to incorporate positive thinking into your life.

This book is for anyone who is looking to cultivate a positive attitude and achieve success. Whether you are a student, a professional, or a business owner, this book will provide the insight and tools you need to reach your goals. By the time you finish this book, you will have a better understanding of the power of positive thinking and how to use it to your advantage.

I

Understanding Positive Thinking - What it is and why it's important

Positive thinking is a mental and emotional attitude that focuses on the good and expects results that will benefit you. It is about looking at the world with optimism and hope, instead of dwelling on the negatives. Positive thinking can have a profound impact on our lives, allowing us to achieve greater success and satisfaction.

In order to understand positive thinking, it's important to recognize the power of our thoughts and how they affect our lives. Our thoughts can have either positive or negative effects, depending on the attitude and perspective we take. Positive thinking can help us to make better decisions, focus on the good, and stay motivated in challenging situations.

Positive thinking also has many benefits for our physical and mental health. Studies have shown that optimistic people are more likely to enjoy better physical health, as well as better mental health. They are less likely to suffer from depression and anxiety, and they also have better coping skills and greater resistance to illness.

Positive thinking also helps us to become better problem-solvers and decision-makers. When we think positively, we are more likely to take productive actions instead of getting stuck in negative thought patterns. We are better able to see the opportunities in any situation, and we can use our creative problem-solving skills to find solutions.

Finally, positive thinking can help us to develop a more positive outlook on life. When we are optimistic about our future, we are more likely to achieve our goals and enjoy greater success. We can also develop stronger relationships with others, as our positive attitude will help us to connect with people in more meaningful ways.

Positive thinking is an essential skill to have in order to live a successful and fulfilling life. It can help us to stay motivated and focused on the good, while also having a positive impact on our physical and mental health. Learning to think positively is an ongoing process, but the benefits are well worth the effort.

"The more you know yourself, the less you are prone to making ethical mistakes."
- J.C. Watts

ഩ

II

Overcoming Negative Thoughts - Recognizing and Changing Negative Thought Patterns

Negative thoughts can be a powerful force in our lives, leading to feelings of depression, hopelessness, and low self-esteem. Fortunately, there are steps we can take to recognize and change these negative thought patterns.

The first step is to recognize when our thoughts are negative. This can seem difficult at first, but the more aware we become of our thoughts, the easier it becomes to identify them. Once we become aware of our negative thoughts, we can start to challenge them.

One way to challenge our negative thoughts is to ask ourselves if they are true. If the answer is no, then we can start to look for evidence to support the opposite thought. For example, if we have the thought that "I am a failure", we can look for evidence that we have accomplished things in our lives.

Another way to challenge negative thoughts is to use reframing. Reframing involves looking at a situation from a different perspective. This can help us to put our current situation in a more positive light.

We can also practice self-compassion when dealing with negative thoughts. Self-compassion involves being kind and understanding toward ourselves, instead of being overly critical.

Finally, it's important to remember that negative thoughts can be a normal part of life. We can't always control them, but we can learn to recognize and manage them. With practice, we can learn to replace our negative thoughts with more positive and empowering ones.

In conclusion, overcoming negative thoughts is not easy, but it is possible. By recognizing and challenging our negative thoughts, using reframing, and practicing self-compassion, we can learn to move past our negative thoughts and live happier and more fulfilling life.

"The only way to do great work is to love what you do. If you haven't found it yet, keep looking."
- Steve Jobs

ꕤ

III

Developing a Positive Attitude - Strategies for Creating a Positive Outlook

Developing a positive attitude can be a challenge, but it's worth the effort. A positive attitude can help us to feel more confident, motivated, and productive. It can also help us to build better relationships and create a more meaningful life.

The first step to developing a positive attitude is to recognize our negative thoughts and behaviors. This can be difficult, but it is the only way to start the process of changing our attitude. Once we've identified our negative thoughts and behaviors, we can begin to replace them with more positive ones.

One way to do this is to practice positive self-talk. Positive self-talk involves talking to ourselves in a kind, encouraging way. This can help us to develop a more positive outlook on life.

Another way to develop a positive attitude is to practice gratitude. Taking the time to appreciate what we have can help us to reframe our perspective and appreciate the good in our lives.

It is also important to focus on the present moment. Being mindful of the present can help us to stay in the moment and appreciate the beauty of life.

Finally, it is important to spend time with positive people. Surrounding ourselves with positive people can help us to stay motivated and inspired.

Developing a positive attitude takes practice, but the benefits are worth the effort. By recognizing our negative thoughts and behaviors, practicing positive self-talk, being grateful, staying mindful, and spending time with positive people, we can develop a more positive outlook on life.

"Happiness is not something ready made. It comes from your own actions."
- Dalai Lama

৪৩

IV

Visualization and Affirmations - Using visualizations and positive affirmations to strengthen your positive outlook

Visualization and affirmations are powerful tools to help us create a more positive outlook on life. Visualization involves creating mental images of our desired outcomes and the life we want to live. Affirmations are positive statements that we repeat to ourselves to help us create new thought patterns and behaviors.

Visualization helps us to access the power of our subconscious mind and tap into the creative energy of the universe. By visualizing our goals, we can create a sense of clarity and focus that will help us take the necessary steps to make our dreams a reality.

Affirmations can help us to change our negative thought patterns and create new ones. They can also help us to stay motivated and inspired to take action. Repeating affirmations every day can help us to create a new internal dialogue and create a more positive outlook on life.

Using both visualizations and affirmations can help us to focus on the good in our lives and create a more positive attitude. They help us to stay focused on our goals and keep our minds open to any opportunities that come our way.

Visualization and affirmations are powerful tools to help us create a more positive outlook on life. By visualizing the life we want to live and repeating affirmations every day, we can create a more positive internal dialogue and stay focused on our goals.

"The greatest glory in living lies not in never falling, but in rising every time we fall."
- Nelson Mandela

☙

V

Managing Stress - Learning to manage stress and reduce its negative effects

Managing stress is an important part of leading a healthy and productive life. Stress can have a negative effect on our physical and mental health, so it's important to learn how to manage it.

One way to manage stress is to recognize the signs of stress and take steps to reduce it. Common signs of stress include difficulty sleeping, irritability, difficulty concentrating, and muscle tension. Taking time out to relax and practice deep breathing can help to reduce stress levels.

Another way to manage stress is to create healthy boundaries. Setting boundaries can help us to take control of our lives and focus on our own needs. It's important to be clear about what is and isn't acceptable in our relationships and to take time for ourselves.

It's also important to recognize when we're feeling overwhelmed and practice self-care. Taking time to do activities that we enjoy can help us to relax and reduce our stress levels.

Finally, it's important to seek help when needed. Talking to a professional counselor can help us to understand our stress and learn new ways to cope with it.

Managing stress is an important part of living a healthy and balanced life. By recognizing the signs of stress, setting healthy boundaries, practicing self-care, and seeking help when needed, we can learn to manage stress and reduce its negative effects.

"The best way to predict your future is to create it."
- Abraham Lincoln

ꕥ

VI

Building Self-Confidence - Strategies to build your self-confidence and Self-Esteem

Building self-confidence and self-esteem is an important part of leading a successful and fulfilling life. Self-confidence is the belief that we have the skills and abilities to achieve our goals and be successful. Self-esteem is the belief that we are worthy and valuable individuals.

There are several strategies that can help us to build our self-confidence and self-esteem. One strategy is to practice positive self-talk. Positive self-talk involves talking to ourselves in a kind and encouraging way. This can help us to view ourselves in a more positive light and boost our self-confidence.

Another strategy is to set realistic goals. Setting realistic goals can help us to stay motivated and focused on what we want to achieve. It can also help us to build our self-confidence and self-esteem when we reach our goals.

It's also important to recognize and celebrate our successes. Taking the time to recognize our successes can help us to feel proud of our accomplishments and boost our self-esteem.

Finally, it's important to practice self-care. Taking care of our physical and mental health can help us to feel better about ourselves and increase our self-confidence.

Building self-confidence and self-esteem is an important part of leading a successful and fulfilling life. By practicing positive self-talk, setting realistic goals, recognizing and celebrating our successes, and practicing self-care, we can build our self-confidence and self-esteem.

"The only limit to our realization of tomorrow will be our doubts of today."
- Franklin D. Roosevelt

ꕥ

VII

Increasing Your Motivation - Tips for increasing motivation and taking action

Increasing motivation is an important part of achieving our goals and creating the life we want. Motivation helps us to take action and make progress, so it's important to learn how to increase our motivation levels.

One way to increase motivation is to set specific and achievable goals. Setting clear and realistic goals can help us to stay focused on what we want to achieve and take action.

Another way to increase motivation is to break down our goals into smaller steps. Breaking down our goals into smaller, more manageable tasks can help us to stay focused and motivated.

It's also important to reward ourselves. Taking the time to celebrate our successes can help us to stay motivated and recognize our progress.

Finally, it's important to create an environment that is conducive to success. Taking the time to organize our workspace and create a positive atmosphere can help us to stay motivated and take action.

Increasing motivation is an important part of achieving our goals and creating the life we want. By setting specific and achievable goals, breaking down our goals into smaller steps, rewarding ourselves, and creating an environment that is conducive to success, we can increase our motivation and take action.

"Positive anything is better than negative nothing." - Elbert Hubbard

ℬ

VIII

Developing Positive Relationships - Building Strong Relationships With Those Around You

Developing positive relationships with those around us is an important part of leading a successful and fulfilling life. Positive relationships can help us to feel connected and supported, and can provide us with opportunities for growth and development.

One way to develop positive relationships is to take the time to get to know the people around us. Taking the time to listen to and learn about others can help us to build meaningful relationships.

Another way to develop positive relationships is, to be honest and open with others. Being honest and open about our thoughts and feelings can help us to build trust and foster positive relationships.

It's also important to be respectful and supportive of others. Taking the time to recognize and celebrate the successes of those around us can help us to build strong relationships.

Finally, it's important to take responsibility for our own actions. Taking the time to think about our words and actions can help us to build positive relationships.

Developing positive relationships with those around us is an important part of leading a successful and fulfilling life. By taking the time to get to know the people around us, being honest and open, being respectful and supportive, and taking responsibility for our own actions, we can build strong relationships with those around us.

"When one door of happiness closes, another opens, but often we look so long at the closed door that we do not see the one that has been opened for us."

- Helen Keller

ꕤ

IX

Understanding The Power Of Gratitude - Learning The Power Of Gratitude And How To Cultivate It

Understanding the power of gratitude is essential for leading a successful and fulfilling life. Gratitude is a powerful emotion that can have a positive impact on our lives. It can help us to focus on the good things in our lives, and to appreciate the blessings we have been given.

One way to understand the power of gratitude is to take the time to recognize our blessings. Taking the time to reflect on the good things in our lives can help us to cultivate gratitude.

Another way to understand the power of gratitude is to practice expressing it. Taking the time to say thank you to those around us can help us to cultivate gratitude and express our appreciation.

It's also important to keep a gratitude journal. Taking the time to write down our blessings can help us to stay focused on the good things in our lives and cultivate gratitude.

Finally, it's important to practice mindfulness. Taking the time to be mindful of our thoughts and feelings can help us to stay present in the moment and cultivate gratitude.

Understanding the power of gratitude is essential for leading a successful and fulfilling life. By taking the time to recognize our blessings, practice expressing it, keep a gratitude journal, and practice mindfulness, we can learn the power of gratitude and how to cultivate it.

"Believe in yourself and all that you are. Know that there is something inside you that is greater than any obstacle."

ꕥ

X

The Habits Of Successful People - Examining The Habits And Traits Of Successful People

Examining the habits and traits of successful people is a great way to learn about how to achieve success. Successful people tend to have certain habits and traits that set them apart from the rest.

One habit of successful people is setting clear and achievable goals. Taking the time to plan and set specific, realistic goals can help us to stay focused and motivated.

Another habit of successful people is hard work. Successful people understand that hard work is essential for achieving their goals. They have the discipline to work hard and stay focused, even when the going gets tough.

It's also important to practice self-reflection. Taking the time to reflect on our thoughts and feelings can help us to stay present in the moment and make better decisions.

Finally, successful people tend to be resilient. They understand that failure is part of the journey and use it as an opportunity to grow and improve.

Examining the habits and traits of successful people is a great way to learn about how to achieve success. By setting clear and achievable goals, practicing hard work, practicing self-reflection, and practicing resilience, we can learn from the habits and traits of successful people.

"The only limit to our realization of tomorrow will be our doubts of today."

ꕤ

XI

Taking Action - Developing An Action Plan For Success And Implementation

Developing an action plan is an essential part of achieving success. An action plan is a step-by-step plan of how to reach a goal. It outlines the tasks and resources that need to be completed in order to reach the desired outcome.

One way to develop an action plan is to set SMART goals. Taking the time to set specific, measurable, achievable, realistic, and time-bound goals can help us to stay focused and motivated.

Another way to develop an action plan is to create a list of tasks. Taking the time to identify all of the tasks that need to be completed can help us to stay organized and on track.

It's also important to allocate resources. Taking the time to allot the right resources, like team members, project budget, or necessary equipment, can help us to stay on target and make sure our action plan is successful.

Finally, it's important to prioritize tasks and set deadlines. Taking the time to highlight important tasks and set deadlines can help us to stay focused and motivated.

Developing an action plan is an essential part of achieving success. By setting SMART goals, creating a list of tasks, allocating resources, and prioritizing tasks, and setting deadlines, we can develop an action plan for success and implementation.

Other Books Of The Author

1. The Moments When I Met God
2. Kashiyile Theertha Pathangal
3. GURU GYAN VANI
4. Abhiprerak Gita
5. ASSI SE JAIN GHAT TAK
6. Hopelessness of Arjuna
7. The Soul and It's True Nature
8. Sense of Action (Karma)
9. Action through Wisdom
10. Action through Wisdom
11. THEORY AND PRACTICAL OF EVERY ACTION
12. LOGICAL UNDERSTANDING OF THE SUPREME
13. THE IMPERISHABLE SUPREME
14. Yatra Nishadraj se Hanuman Ghat Tak
15. Yatra Karnatak Ghat se Raja Ghat Tak
16. Yatra Pandey Ghat se Prayagraj Ghat Tak
17. Yatra Ranjendra Prasad Ghat se Dattatreya Ghat Tak
18. YaatraSindhiya Ghat se Gwaliar Ghat Tak
19. Yatra Mangala Gauri Ghat se Hanuman Gadhi Ghat Tak
20. Yatra Gaay Ghat Se Nishad Ghat Tak
21. MAA GANGA, GHATEN EVM UTSAV
22. Ganga Arti Dev Deepavali evam Any Utsav
23. Potentials of Digitalized India
24. VEDIC CONSCIOUSNESS
25. A Brief Introduction to Vedic Science
26. Kashi ke Barah Jyotirling
27. IMPACT OF MOTIVATION
28. Let's have a Milky Way Journey
29. Color Therapy in a Nutshell

30. Rigveda in a Nutshell
31. Yajurveda in a Nutshell
32. Samveda in a Nutshell
33. Atharva Veda in a Nutshell
34. Ayushman Bhava - Ayurveda
35. Srimad Bhagavad Gita and Upanishad Connection
36. Srimad Bhagavad Gita - an attempt to summarize each chapter.
37. Facts and Impact of Nakshatra
38. Astro Gems - NAVARATNA
39. Ekadashi - A Concise Overview
40. A Concise View of Hanuman Chalisa
41. Inspirational Gita
42. Nakshatraranyam
43. Summary of 18 Mahapuranas
44. Synopsis of 18 Upa Puranas
45. Rigvediya Upanishads
46. Shukla Yajurvediya Upanishads
47. Krishna Yajurvediya Upanishads
48. Samavediya Upanishads
49. Atharvavediya Upanishads
50. The Seven Great Sages
51. From Rocket Scientist to President Dr. APJ Abdul Kalam
52. The Visionary's Voice - Quotes of Dr. APJ Abdul Kalam
53. The Wisdom of Swami Vivekananda: Insights and Inspiration from a Legendary Spiritual Teacher
54. Ayurvedic Remedies from the Garden
55. Sages and Seers
56. Rising Strong – Motivational Stories of Women
57. Beyond Flames -Mystery stories of Funeral Ghat Manikarnika
58. The Origins of Tulsi: A Look at the Mythological Roots of the Plant"

59. The Holistic Cow: A Look at the Physical, Spiritual, and Cultural Importance of Cows in India
60. Arts of Healing
61. Exploring the Divine
62. Understanding Five Elements
63. The Etymology of Ram
64. Symbols of India
65. Voice of Change (About Speeches of Great Men)
66. She Speaks (About Speeches of Great Women)
67. Patriotism on Celluloid – Brief About Patriotic Films
68. The Music of Motivation: A Brief Guide to Inspirational Film Songs
69. **Unlocking the Secrets of the Dashopanishads**
70. A Cultural Mosaic
71. Ancient Traditions, Modern Minds
72. Ecos of Ancient Wisdom
73. Beneath the Surface
74. From Temples to Ashrams
75. Sages of the Subcontinent
76. The Art of Healling (Ayurveda, Yoga & Naturopathy)
77. Indian Kitchen
78. The Festivals of India
79. The Indian Epics Retold
80. The Power of Mantras
81. The Indian River Ganges
82. The Indian Architecture
83. Rites of Passage
84. The Indian Silk Road
85. The Indian Literature
86. The Indian Villages
87. The Indian Folks & Crafts
88. The Way of Buddha
89. The Ramayan of Tulsidas

90. Astrological Remedies
91. The Secret Power of Motivation
92. Secret of Developing your Inner Strength
93. The Secret Path to Motivation
94. The Art and Secret of Positive Thinking
95. The Secrets of Practicing Ethical Living
96. Indian Art and Painting
97. The Indian Herbalism
98. Bharatanatyam to Kathak
99. Exploring India's Astrological Remedies

CONTACT

DR. JAGADEESH PILLAI

PhD in Vedic Science

Four Times Guinness World Record Holder

Winner of Mahatma Gandhi Vishwa Shanti Puraskar and Global Peace Ambassador

Gemology, Astro & Vastu Consultant - Spiritual Counselor

Consultant for designing World Record Ideas

Efficient Tarot Card Reader

9839093003

myrichindia@gmail.com

drjagadeeshpillai@facebook

drjagadeeshpillai@instagram

jagadeeshpillai@youtube

www. JAGADEESHPILLAI.com

|| LOKAHA SAMASTHAHA SUKHINO BHAVANTU ||

9 798889 513629

Printed by Libri Plureos GmbH in Hamburg,
Germany